JESUS ALIVE IN OUR LIVES

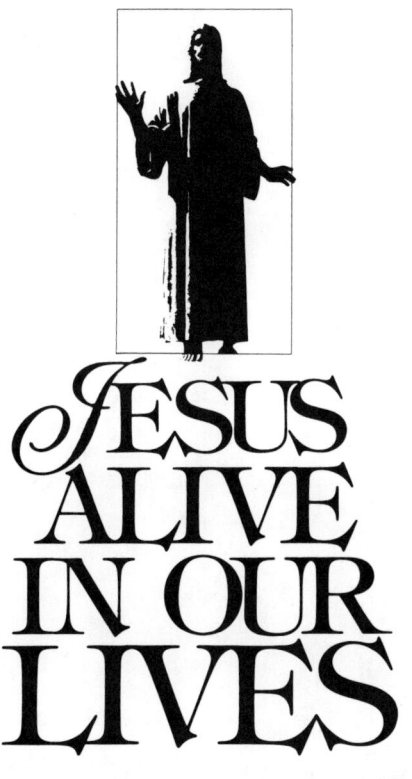

JESUS ALIVE IN OUR LIVES

Philip A. St. Romain

AVE MARIA PRESS Notre Dame, Indiana 46556

© 1985 by Ave Maria Press

All rights reserved. No part of this publication may be reproduced, stored in a retrieval system, or transmitted, in any form or by any means, electronic, mechanical, photocopying, recording, or otherwise, without the written permission of the publisher, Ave Maria Press, Notre Dame, Indiana 46556.

Library of Congress Catalog Card Number: 85-71676

International Standard Book Number: 0-87793-293-X

Cover art: "Christ the Teacher" sculpture at the entrance of Merrimack College, North Andover, Massachusetts. Photo by David Powell.

Cover and text design: Katherine A. Robinson

Printed and bound in the United States of America.

To all scientists and other seekers of truth: that they may come to believe in the resurrection of the Lord of all truth.

Contents

	Acknowledgments	11
	Introduction	13
One	The Witness of the Church	19
Two	Incarnation: God Is With Us	35
Three	New Life	43
Four	The Mystical Body	51
Five	When Good Things Happen to Bad People	57
Six	Courage to Live	67
Seven	The Meaning of Suffering	73
Eight	Meaning in Life	81
Nine	The Reign of God	87
	Appendix One: Questions for Reflection and Discussion	97
	Appendix Two: Suggested Reading	101

Acknowledgments

Like so many other books, this one began with a question. During the course of my campus ministry days at Louisiana State University, I was asked to give a talk to students on the meaning of the resurrection. This forced me to take a good, hard look at the status of my own beliefs, and prompted the memories disclosed in the Introduction. I would like to thank the students from that Awakening Retreat community for the many opportunities and challenges they extended to me through the years.

We live at a time in history when biblical scholarship is richer than ever. Many of the ideas in this book derive from the researches of Raymond Brown, Roland Murphy, John McKenzie, Hans Kung, Karl Rahner, and Avery Dulles, to name a few. A small book on the resurrection by Thomas Merton also deserves special mention here.

Many thanks to Father John Edmonds, S.T., Father Dan Drinan, C.M.F., Shirley Smith and Philip Sheridan for reading this manuscript and providing helpful feedback. Frank Cunningham and the editorial staff at Ave Maria Press also provided direction and encouragement through several drafts of the manuscript.

Finally, I acknowledge my indebtedness to Lisa, my wife, for her editorial and moral support. Without her help, this book could have never been written.

Introduction

Why another book about the resurrection of Jesus of Nazareth?

It would be an understatement to say that much has already been written about this most significant of Christian beliefs.

In order to answer this question, I feel compelled to share a bit of my own journey in faith. About 12 years ago, I attended a Cursillo and was deeply moved by the experience. As a biology graduate student and somewhat of an agnostic at that time, my training in science led me to search out credible evidence for the resurrection to bring my mind into sync with my almost embarrassingly enthusiastic heart. I read the scriptures with an open mind and was deeply moved by the teachings of Jesus and the story of his passion and death. I was unimpressed by the resurrection stories, however. There seemed to be contradictions among the evangelists as to who the witnesses were, where the appearances took place, whether or not there was a guard.

Like most Catholics when confused about religious matters, I turned to my local parish priest, in this case an extraordinarily well-educated campus minister. He told me he doubted that Jesus' corpse was transformed to new life and he surmised that the empty tomb passages were probably mythological stories with no historical rootings. This was quite disconcerting, but like a good scientist I was prepared to believe the truth even if it was unpleasant. But why, I asked myself, should I take the word of only one man on so important a topic? I would have to study and make up my own mind; that much was for sure.

The very next day I bought a copy of Raymond Brown's book, *The Virginal Conception and Bodily Resurrection of Jesus*. It was not easy reading! I followed the gist of his research as best I could and found myself surprisingly pleased with his affirmation of the traditional dogmas regarding these matters. My mind gave my heart permission to remain excited about the spiritual life, and so I scheduled an appointment to meet with my campus minister again. He did not seem surprised by Brown's conclusions, but told me that it was more important to reflect upon the *meaning* of the resurrection than upon the event itself. I have since come to agree with him, although when I left his office that day I felt he had been evasive and even dishonest with me.

My problem was quite simple. It was impossible for me to allow myself to grapple with the meaning of an event that might have been *only* mythological. If Jesus did not really rise from the dead, then the resurrection has no real meaning other than its poetic comment on the life of a great man. I might just as well have dusted off my old Greek mythology texts as studied the Bible; the Greeks wrote fascinating myths and promoted a values system close to the one I had already embraced. With my biology peers exerting considerable pressure for me to abandon the resurrection question (or else to use religion simply as a social outlet, which a few did themselves), I soon became tormented

INTRODUCTION

by a severe existential crisis, the center of which concerned the mystery of Jesus.

In addition to my thesis research (on the evolution of two mouse species), I began reading everything I could get my hands on about Jesus, thus hoping to cast off conclusively or embrace the tenuous strands of faith remaining in my heart. What I found was that there are three types of books about the resurrection; each made its own unique contributions in helping me to grow in my understanding of Jesus and the church:

1. *Devotional* treatments take the fact of the resurrection for granted, focusing instead on its meaning for those who follow Jesus.

2. *Dogma* deals with the theological implications of the resurrection, i.e., how we are to understand what the risen Christ reveals to us about God and humanity. In most cases, dogmatic theologians begin with the fact of the resurrection and spend little time investigating its nature.

3. *Exegeses* of scripture are examinations of how the Bible is put together and what it is saying. When applied to the resurrection narratives, however, the various types of biblical criticism (redactionary, literary, historical, etc.) sometimes leave one wondering if the sacred writings are rooted in any historical substrate at all! Some, like Raymond Brown, conclude that the resurrection narratives in scripture do point to miraculous appearances of the once-crucified Jesus to his band of stunned followers. Others turn the narratives into mere mythology.

I sincerely wish there had been a fourth category of books more available at that time; science and the resurrection would have been just what I needed to read about, for it was squaring the resurrection with the scientific world-view that gave me my most intense headaches. If, for example, we are saying that the body of Jesus was transformed to new life—that his tomb was really empty on Easter Sunday—then what are we saying might have happened to his body? (A less interesting, but intriguing question might be raised concerning the microorganisms in his body.) It is one thing to claim that a man's spirit has risen, for this would not be a debatable matter; it is another thing entirely to claim that a corpse has been not just resuscitated, but completely transformed so that it can no longer die. To state simply that God did it, or else that we do not know and need not trouble over such matters is to shun dialogue with a predominantly agnostic group of very influential people—namely, scientists. Many scientists are exceedingly impervious to persuasive appeals based on emotionalism or claims of the miraculous. All scientists (and non-scientists) know, too, that dead people usually remain dead. If, therefore, we would like scientists to be active participants in a world religion that owes its origin to the resurrection of a dead man, then we must at least be willing to discuss with them any scientific questions implied by the resurrection. These people are not nearly so close-minded as some might imagine, for the emerging post-Einsteinian world-view is nowhere near as smug in its view of the possibilities in nature as were the Newtonians. At any rate, such discussions and reflections would have helped me out considerably—and still would, I believe.

    I must confess that I have never been able to explain the resurrection of Jesus using a scientific approach. Nevertheless, I emerged from those grad student crisis days a believer, and have been since. Like

Introduction

most Christians, I suppose, my faith has surfaced from a variety of roots. A simple apologetics of sorts finally stabilized my mind and allowed me to become convinced that one could be intellectually honest and believe, and still not understand everything. This is, after all, the way we comprehend much of the world, and is also the state of science as a whole. It was essential for me that faith not demand irrationality, for the lessons of history clearly point to grave consequences for individuals and societies that abandon the light of human reason.

More than on apologetics, however, my faith has come to rest in a growing conviction that *Jesus Christ is alive in my life*. I know that when I pray, something amazing happens inside of me that is qualitatively different from when I just sit quietly, or read a book, or do anything else; I know that in the depths of my being I am not alone; finally, I know that when I live as Christ calls me to, I am happy. This is enough to dispel most of my residual agnosticism most of the time. Perhaps there will come a day when physicists will be able to identify dimensions of reality that at once embrace and transcend space-time as a sphere does a mere circle. I believe they eventually *must*, for I am convinced that Jesus lives in such a dimension, and that at least part of our minds are in touch with it.

About This Book

I have written this book to try to make more accessible some of the studies and reflections concerning the resurrection of Jesus that I have been privileged to read. Because this topic is so central to Christian belief, I hope to help focus for believers as well as nonbelievers the world-view and lifestyle implied by the life, death and resurrection of Jesus. As the reader will see, belief in the resurrection can make a tremendous difference in how one perceives and copes with several of life's most challenging issues.

Chapter One will be an attempt to summarize briefly what the Bible (hence, the church) and science can and cannot tell us about the resurrection experience of the apostles and the early church. It is a chapter for the mind, and hopefully it will whet the reader's appetite for the more scholarly works listed at the end of this book.

Chapters Two to Nine will focus on the meaning of the resurrection. They are reflections for the mind, but also for the heart and the will. In truth, the resurrection was never intended to be an idle belief, but a lived-out experience.

Reflection/discussion questions for each of these chapters are included in an appendix to help the reader internalize and digest the various topics covered. Writing in a personal journal, dialoguing with a spiritual director and discussing the book in a group are also ways to help the subject matter come alive.

One

The Witness of the Church

We should be guilty of extreme dullness if we did not marvel at times that the church is the only institution in the world that centers its life and activities on the premise that a man who lived about 2,000 years ago is still living and involved in the affairs of humanity. Ironically, this institution, which makes such fantastic claims about Jesus of Nazareth, is passionately dedicated to promoting sanity and clear thinking.

Yet everything we know about Jesus of Nazareth comes to us from the church. Unfortunately, there are no accounts from non-Christian sources contemporary to Jesus' times that give us anything more than what the church was already saying about the man. What we know about Jesus we know from the writings of late first-generation and early second-generation followers. Those writings, considered to be authoritative and in keeping with traditions already firmly established at that time (50–100 A.D.), were accepted as canonical; they are the writings we today call the New Testament.

But what does this New Testament really tell us about Jesus? Anyone who reads its chapters will find them decidedly sympathetic toward Jesus and his teachings. This strong element of subjective bias is admitted by responsible scripture scholars of all Christian denominations. It is obvious that the evangelists and St. Paul believed very strongly that Jesus was the Messiah long awaited by the Jews. What kind of objective truths might we expect from such authors?

Fortunately, we have learned quite a lot about the culture and the history of the Roman Empire's Middle East during the past century. Much of this can help us to understand customs and practices that might seem strange to us today. The Roman method of crucifixion, for example, is described in many non-Christian writings, all of which suggest that the biblical account of the crucifixion of Jesus is fairly true to the usual procedure. We are also more knowledgeable of the peculiar political relationship which existed between the Jews and the Romans—an arrangement which necessitated collaboration between both parties in the death of Jesus.

Historical criticism has helped us to realize that there is much about Jesus in scripture that comes with the clarity of hindsight. After Pentecost, the followers of Jesus retold stories about him with a deeper understanding of the events of his life than when those events first occurred. The feeding of the multitudes, for example, eventually became a symbol for the Bread of Life who was broken and whose blood was poured out for all. It is certain that Jesus' disciples missed this point at the time it happened.

Form and literary criticism have taught us that we had best consider the kind of writing we are dealing with when pondering the meaning of scripture. In scripture we find poetry, parables, letters (epistles), prayers, genealogies, apocalyptic writings and myths. All of these literary forms of expression reveal truth, but the content of that truth cannot be understood without considering its literary context. Who, for example, would take literally John's description of Jesus found in the Book of Revelation? We all know that in making his point about the birds in the sky Jesus must have known that many birds do in fact die of starvation every day. No one takes the parables as literal explanations but as symbolic inferences of what God's kingdom is all about; I, for one, would be sorely disappointed if heaven turned out to be a gigantic batch of leavening dough (see Mt 13:33). The Word of God comes to us in human words, and we need to keep that in mind when studying scripture.

What the Scriptures Are

If all we know about Jesus comes to us from the church, and if the church's remembrance of Jesus as found in scripture is interpreted by faith, then what, might we ask, can we know about what Jesus really did and said among us?

As the early Christian community grew in its understanding of Jesus as the Messiah whose life, teachings, death and resurrection fulfilled countless prophecies of old, it was natural that this understanding would accompany narration of the naked, historical facts about Jesus' life. If the writers of scripture were posing as historical scientists, we could fault them on this point. What we have, instead, is a loving, faith-filled memory of the key events in Jesus' life with a fuller understanding of the meaning of those events.

The scriptures were written by people of faith to provoke faith and to deepen religious insight. They never attempt to present themselves otherwise. Historical, mythical and theological data in scripture are true in the sense that they honestly express the understanding of the significance of the life of Jesus held by the early church.

The scriptures are not writings about history in the 20th-century sense of the term. There is a tremendous neglect for historical and biographical details among all of the authors of the New Testament. Why, we do not even know what Jesus looked like! Mark's gospel, the earliest of the four, neglects any mention of his origins; none of the writings tells us anything significant about his education—something that would seem to be of interest when discussing a spiritual genius like Jesus. Contemporary biographers must find these omissions appalling!

In the same breath, however, we must be quick to acknowledge that scripture is not entirely ahistorical. Strewn throughout its pages are names of people whose existence can be confirmed by nonbiblical sources. Scripture is generally true to geography and seldom poses events to have taken place in the wrong time. We do know that Jesus has a definite place in history; he was born during the reign of Augustus and died during the reign of Tiberius. A few names and places jotted down as asides by the evangelists let on this much.

From the foregoing it should now be clear that

scripture does not permit an accurate formulation of a biography of Jesus (even though many such books have been written). Events from his life preserved for us were written down because of their meaning to the early church. As the appendix to John's gospel states in a moment of historical fidelity: "There are still many other things that Jesus did, yet if they were written down in detail, I doubt there would be room enough in the entire world to hold the books to record them" (Jn 21:25 NAB). Let us, therefore, expect no more from scripture than scripture proposes to give: a quasi-historical account of the meaning of certain events in the life of Jesus of Nazareth.

Scripture and the Resurrection

In this book we are considering the evidence for and the significance of the resurrection of Jesus. Given the nature of scripture described above, what evidence for the resurrection can be gleaned from the New Testament?

Upon reading the resurrection accounts in the gospels and in Paul's letters, we will immediately note their insistence upon the possibility of living a new life in the Spirit. This possibility, for them, derives from the crucifixion and resurrection of Jesus of Nazareth (see Rom 8:1-11). It is apparent that they view this resurrection as more than a merely symbolic or poetic way of referring to the advancement of the Christian way of life. In the New Testament, the spread of Christian values is explained as a consequence of the work of the risen Jesus, and not vice versa.

The origin of the church can be traced to the testimonies of those who claimed that Jesus rose from the dead. This faith still forms the unifying center of Christian beliefs and practices. It would, therefore, seem reasonable to inquire first of all what exactly the church is proposing for our consideration, and, secondly, the evidence in favor of her sacred message. What, in other words, does the church mean when speaking about the resurrection, and why should we take this belief seriously?

When attempting to comprehend the nature of Jesus' resurrection as described by the church in scripture, one immediately notices the conspicuous absence of any clear, objective evidence for it. No one saw him rise, and one wishes that Jesus would have followed his own earlier counsel and shown himself to the priests. Furthermore, there is disagreement among the narratives as to when he appeared, and where, and to whom, and what he did and said on those occasions. As might be expected, critics of Christianity have long called attention to these inconsistencies, insinuating that the authors got their contrivances mixed up.

Confusing though the resurrection accounts in scripture might be, it is certain that they are not mixed-up contrivances. Matthew and Luke wrote their testaments with Mark in hand, and the author of John must certainly have been aware of the other gospels when he wrote his exalted work over 25 years later. If anything, the differences in the four gospels are intentional, and not the consequence of confusion and forgetfulness. Scholars have pointed out that the discrepancies are consistent with the themes developed by the authors throughout the whole of their works.

If we put aside the differences in characters, places and activities in the resurrection narratives and focus instead on the experience of encounter with the risen Jesus described therein, we find the gospels consistent in emphasizing the following points:

1. The empty tomb passages show that the risen one experienced was Jesus of Nazareth and not someone else. They also suggest that there was no evidence which could be used by critics to refute the resurrection.

2. The encounter was with no ghost or mere figment of the imagination. The verses describing meals together are attempts to bring this point home (after the risen one left, there were scraps on the plate).

3. The risen one was not merely a resuscitated Jesus animating the same mortal corpse. Unlike Lazarus, whom Jesus raised from the dead, Jesus would never die again; he had conquered death forever.

4. The risen one revealed himself in a very special way to only a small, elect group. Their experience of him was much more profound than was that enjoyed by those who believed on their words.

5. The risen one did not return to bring vengeance to bear against his executioners, but to augment an age of reconciliation and forgiveness.

After all is said and done, these common points speak more in favor of a similarity of experience among the apostles than the differences in the stories do against. Although expressed in a variety of ways, the resurrection narratives all remain faithful to what must have already been a stable consensus of opinion regarding the apostles' encounter with the risen Jesus. We are aware, today, of variations among the stories of individuals who all witness the same phenomenon; how much more can we expect differences in relating experiences of the ineffable. The miracle is that these narratives are as similar as they are!

Historical Considerations

Now that we have a better idea as to what the church is proposing we believe about the resurrection, it is time to ask in earnest just why anyone should give serious consideration to so preposterous a claim. Because I do not believe that blind, unquestioning faith is a very great Christian virtue, and because I know that reason must be at least partially converted if one's faith is to be real, I have found it important in my own life to examine the scriptures with a view to glean from them whatever historical or circumstantial evidence that might help to substantiate its claims. This used to be not so difficult, since the scriptures were simply interpreted literally. Apologetics were comparatively simple when one considered the stories of the empty tomb with its guards, angels, mystified women and earthquakes to be historical facts without qualifications. Many Fundamentalist Christians (e.g., Josh McDowell) still accept all that is written about the resurrection in scripture to be historical in nature, but scholars from the mainline Christian denominations assure us that the literal historicity of these accounts is doubtful. Whatever historical experiences underpin them are difficult to grasp with certainty, since they have all become so thoroughly embellished with legendary and theological elements as to cloud over the initial experiences.

We need not lay aside our Bibles as mere mythologies yet, however; there is still a great deal of history left intact by the critics—enough to formulate the simple apologetics enumerated below:

1. *Jesus of Nazareth lived* in the Middle East sometime between 4 B.C. and 30 A.D. He was certainly a Jew and an extraordinary enough person to attract a sizeable following. This merited him the scorn of the

religious leaders of his day. The sheer number of healings attributed to him also points to a very special ministry of making people whole.

2. *Jesus of Nazareth was crucified.* Death by Roman crucifixion was considered scandalous; it is doubtful that the early church would have sought to ennoble its hero by inventing such a death for him. Furthermore, the procedure used to execute Jesus that is outlined in the passion narratives is referred to by Paul and other later writers, and seems never to have been denied by the persecutors of the church.

3. *Jesus' corpse was laid in a known gravesite.* We are on shakier ground now, for scholars have identified numerous mythological and legendary elements in the passages concerning the empty tomb. Nevertheless, several factors still attest to a known gravesite. First of all, the tradition of Jesus being buried in the tomb of Joseph of Arimathea: Why should it not be true? Secondly, the accounts of the women visiting the tomb: They would seem to be a faithful recollection, especially since the women's reports (which turned out to be true) were doubted by the future pillars of the church, the apostles. Third, an unknown grave would have allowed the Jews to produce any mutilated corpse and claim that it was Jesus'. As far as we know, the church's persecutors never claimed that Jesus' corpse lay rotting somewhere.

4. *Jesus' tomb was empty Easter morning.* Many exegetes would not be happy with this conclusion, but a couple of considerations render it reasonable. There can be no doubt that Jesus' corpse would have constituted overwhelming evidence against the resurrection, reducing it to a psychic phenomenon open to severe criticism from those outside as well as within

the church. Furthermore, it is difficult to imagine the early Christian martyrs so bravely facing death—all the while knowing that their Master's corpse lay rotting somewhere. For Jewish converts resurrection meant bodily resurrection and no other kind, since to be a person meant to be in the body. That being said, it is important to note that the empty tomb does not of itself prove that Jesus rose from the dead.

5. *The followers of Jesus founded a church based on belief that Jesus rose from the dead.* This ragtag band of fishermen, tax collectors, merchants, prostitutes and down-home country folk—all broken and despairing on Good Friday—became transformed into the world's most courageous people. Something happened to them; they say they met the risen Christ.

These five simple points have withstood the critical scrutiny of scripture scholars and constitute the objective, historical roots of the church. Taken separately, each point means little; taken as a whole, they collectively attest to the reasonableness of belief in the resurrection.

Science and the Resurrection

Religious faith is not simply the product of a process of logical, deductive reasoning such as are the conclusions of science. Faith, by definition, moves beyond evidence into the realm of the unseen and unprovable (see Heb 11:1), rooting itself in hope and trust. Because of this transcendent orientation of faith, many rational agnostics have assumed that faith is anti-rational and close-minded. But science can only examine that within religious experience which can be measured and analyzed with instruments. Moving beyond this space-time world in its focus, Christian faith can never really be verified or denied. The best that science can ever hope to do is to try to explain how the realities affirmed by faith might not be credible.

Christian faith need never be afraid to face the scientific world-view while continuing to affirm its sacred truths. Witnesses of the risen Jesus in the early church never came across as paranoid that they would be caught in a lie. Whatever arguments against the resurrection they encountered were faced with the assurance that nothing could be found which would in any way discredit their faith.

I mentioned in the Introduction that belief in the resurrection is difficult for many scientific-minded people because they cannot comprehend how, given our understanding of nature, Jesus could have risen to new life. The resurrection suggests a wholesale violation of the very laws of nature that scientists usually find operating predictably and consistently. Scientists loathe suspension of nature's laws, for a God who at one moment runs the universe through its laws and the next moment suspends them is a God who removes predictability from the universe. Regarding "miraculous phenomena" such as faith healing and psychokinesis, scientists have sought natural explanations for these phenomena. Regarding the biblical stories of Jesus multiplying fish and loaves, or Jesus walking on water and calming storms, scientists and many contemporary theologians are likely to give a condescending smile and pass these stories off as excessive displays of faith among the early followers of Christ. The resurrection of Jesus is another matter, however, since the existence of the Christian church is a serious matter indeed, owing its origin to belief in the resurrection. And, as we have seen in the previous section, the historical evidence in favor of the resurrection is rationally persuasive, which makes things even more difficult for scientists.

No one ought to be too snobbish concerning our 20th-century view of reality, however. There is much about reality that science does not yet understand. The very origins of the universe remain enshrouded in mystery, as does the origin of life and the nature of mind. Just as our digestive systems and DNA managed to function quite well before we began to learn how they operated, and just as plants turned sunlight into food before we grasped the photosynthetic process, so it may be that we live our lives on the edge of a spiritual universe whose existence our present understanding of physics does not reveal to us. If such a dimension really exists, then our present understanding of the laws of nature will have to eventually take it into account. Perhaps this kind of knowledge is only years away; perhaps it will forever remain accessible only to those who die in Christ and so join him in this new dimension of reality.

There are many who, at this point, will want to interject evidence for this afterlife dimension by referring to the experiences of the clinically dead who "returned to life," or by pointing to spiritual mediums and other esoteric phenomena. This data is not immune to other interpretations, however. For one thing, "afterlife" experiences by the clinically dead are not really afterlife at all; the patients never really died. Those who really die never return to tell about the dark tunnels, beings of light and meetings with deceased relatives that some (but by no means all) of the clinically dead experience. It is not at all clear that the afterlife experiences of the clinically dead are objective experiences of another dimension of reality; perhaps they are only dreamlike hallucinations caused by altered nerve impulse transmission patterns in the brains of people who are close to losing brain function altogether (several researchers have made this point with data to back it). The experiences of psychic mediums are even more suspect; this field is notorious for fraud and deception. At any rate, medium and afterlife experiences give us little clue as to how Jesus could have been raised from the dead.

Maybe this venture of searching out ways in which the resurrection can be squared with science was doomed from the start. What if God, by raising Jesus to new life, did not merely temporarily suspend the laws of nature, but transcended them? *What if the resurrection of Jesus signifies the creation of a new realm of existence, a realm in which Jesus is truly the first-born (see Col :15–20)?* If this is indeed the case, then science will have to wait patiently with the church until this dimension is revealed. For now, let us acknowledge that anyone who believes in the resurrection will have to do so without completely understanding how Jesus could have been raised up, what the nature of his risen body is, etc. Even the apostles were not spared this fate.

What About the Shroud?

Since the Shroud of Turin research team has turned in the results of its late '70s investigations, many people have come to see in this revered relic the most compelling piece of evidence in favor of the resurrection existing today. The research team proved conclusively that the image of the crucified man is not a painting and that the bloodstains are in fact blood. No satisfactory explanation as to how the image could have been made on the cloth has been advanced to date; many of the world's most eminent scientists were stumped on this point after over 100,000 hours of research.

Anyone who has followed Shroud research can only be awed by the religious and scientific implications of this most extraordinary of all relics. The image corresponds in every way to what we know about the crucified Jesus. The Shroud has, in fact, helped us to better contemplate the extreme violence that Roman crucifixion imposed upon subjects. We learned, for example, that contrary to religious artistic depictions of the crucifixion, the nails were driven into the upper wrists between the radius and ulna bones, and not into the metacarpals of the hand, where they would have torn away. Dr. Barbet's book, *A Doctor at Calvary*, provides a moving and penetrating analysis of the medical aspects of crucifixion based on what the Shroud reveals.

Whether the image on the Shroud is or is not that of Jesus of Nazareth will probably never be known. As the Shroud research team put it, there is no scientific test for Jesus. Few people know that the Catholic Church does not officially recognize the Shroud as the burial cloth of Jesus. Unofficial recognition is there, of course, and church authorities in no way discourage veneration of the relic by Catholics. But even if it could be proven that the Shroud of Turin is the authentic burial cloth of Jesus, it would witness more to the crucifixion than to the resurrection. There is the remote possibility that the process which produced the image on the Shroud might give us some insight into the resurrection; several scientists have hypothesized that only a short burst of intense heat could have done so. Still, it is doubtful that we shall ever know with certainty how the image became burned onto the outer fibrils of the linen threads. Like the empty tomb, the Shroud of Turin stands only as a silent or incidental witness to the resurrection.

Conclusions

Where are we then? *What really happened Easter morning?*

All that we can say for sure is that several women and a few men claimed to have encountered the same Jesus of Nazareth crucified a couple of days earlier, but changed now in many wonderful ways. Even the most skeptical among us must at least admit that *they believed they encountered him*. It is the only thing which explains the birth of the church, and it is enough to make our faith credible.

In trying to explain just what might have been the nature of this risen person they encountered, we confront a mystery, a truth which transcends the fullness of our understanding. When confronted with the mystery of the resurrection proclamation, there is little room for diplomatic and compromising responses. Either the resurrection faith is the biggest hoax ever perpetrated upon humanity, or it is God's mysterious work of salvation through the person of Jesus Christ. These are really the only options open to the inquiring mind. Any other evidence for the resurrection will have to be gained from our own experiences in living the life of faith that the church encourages. The mind can take us no further.

Two

The Incarnation: God Is With Us

Throughout history, people have speculated concerning whether or not there is a Higher Power involved in the affairs of humanity and creation. As many ethnologists have discovered, one of our most uniquely human characteristics is our propensity to affirm the existence of this Power, although in many strikingly different ways. It has been the task of religious traditions to describe the nature and intentions of the Divine, and in that vein Christianity is but one of many world religions with something to say about God.

The agnostic looking out over the various world religions will often be tempted to say that religious beliefs are an entirely relative matter. Some people believe that God is detached from and disinterested in creation; then there are other traditions which maintain that God is involved in world affairs, but only in response to our sacrifices and offerings. Those of us in the Judeo-Christian-Islam tradition believe that there is but one God, and that God is passionately interested in what happens on earth. Buddhists and many Hindus do not even like to talk about God, emphasizing instead specific disciplines that help us to live a better life. It is easy to sympathize with agnostics; taken all together, the world's religions pose a varied and often contradictory view of God.

As soon as one begins to grapple with questions concerning God's existence and nature, it becomes imperative to ask how human beings can know anything at all about God. Here again, the world's religious and philosophical traditions tell a confusing story. Some maintain that God is unknowable, and that it does no good whatsoever even to discuss these questions; others maintain that the knowledge of God comes only to a privileged few — priests, shamans and others who are specially initiated into the ways of God. The Jews of Jesus' day believed that only those who kept the Law were capable of knowing God, they despised law breakers because they did not believe God had anything to do with such people (Jn 9:30-34). Many people today act as though they believe that only a high degree of intelligence gives one access to God; this view would withhold knowledge of God from the ignorant and/or uneducated. It's another confusing and muddled picture.

Jesus and the Presence of God

As a result of the resurrection, Christians recognized a special presence of God in the person of Jesus of Nazareth. He was at first identified as the Messiah, the chosen one of God (Mk 8:27–30); then, eventually, as the visible manifestation of the Father (Jn 14:7–11). An early Christian hymn affirmed Jesus' equality with God (Phil 2:6), and Paul maintains that "in Christ the fullness of deity resides in bodily form" (Col 2:9 NAB). How the early Church came to equate Jesus' Messianic role and his oneness with God is a fascinating question, for Jewish tradition did not necessarily hold that the Messiah would be God's Son (much less God himself). For our purposes, we need only recognize the fact that Christians see God in Jesus. We may therefore look to Jesus in order to comprehend what God is like and where God might be found.

If the presence of God is found in the person of Jesus, then we must, even 2,000 years later, continue to marvel at the unlikely places that God has chosen to dwell! Lay theologian Frank Sheed once wrote that the reason the gospel does not touch us is that we read it in a "pious coma." We have heard the stories so many times that we no longer hear them in the proper perspective. Let us, therefore, take a few moments to recount some of the more startling lessons we learn about where God can be found implied in the life of Jesus.

1. *God took on human flesh.* So much for the notion that the body is evil and that our sensual needs are basically sinful! That Christians proclaim Jesus' resurrection to be a bodily resurrection is a further affirmation of the basic goodness of our bodiliness. This belief was influential in helping the early church to understand that the entire physical creation has been sanctified by God, and that nothing shall henceforth be considered unclean. Time and again we meet Jesus

in the gospels as he heals someone's body or even gives them food to eat. The body and its needs are well understood by our human God; never can a Christian justifiably ignore someone's bodily needs for the sake of the kingdom of God. Indeed, our salvation will depend in large part upon how well we have clothed the naked, fed the hungry, comforted the sick and visited the prisoners (Mt 25:31-46).

2. *God is poor.* He did not choose members of the ruling class of ministers and politicians to be his parents; he came into the world through simple ordinary folks. Although exegetes have led us to question the historicity of the infancy narratives, it is still safe to assume that Jesus' birth took place in less than ideal conditions. Like other poor children, he had what his parents, rabbis and other tutors could offer in terms of education, but this was apparently unimpressive to the people of his village (Mt 13:54-58). During his adult ministry, we find him possessing little more than the clothes on his back. "Blessed are the poor," he taught us, practicing what he preached by living a life of poverty and ministering to those neglected in a society that held riches to be a sign of favor from God. He died penniless, wearing only a robe given him in ridicule. Who would have expected this from a god?

3. *God took on ordinary human responsibilities.* He did not turn his back on lowly chores. There is a story about Mahatma Gandhi, and how he reacted to those who refused to clean out the latrines at a community he had founded. This dirty work was normally carried out by a lower caste of Hindus, the untouchables, but Gandhi expected his wife and others in the village to break with the old conventions. We do not know whether or not Jesus cleaned latrines, but there is little

reason to believe that he was spared such chores. In fact, we know very little about the first 30 years of his life—probably there was nothing sensational about them. Joseph, his father, had apparently died before Jesus opened his public ministry, so it may well be that Jesus took on the role as head of the house in the interim years, caring for the needs of his mother and whoever else lived with them. The people of Nazareth called him "the carpenter's son," and tradition has it that he learned this trade and practiced it faithfully. Because Jesus worked, there is no reason for us to believe that any kind of work lacks dignity. Any chore can be a ministry, for God has shown us that he is present even in the ordinary activities of our lives.

4. *Jesus suffered and died.* It is worth noting at this point that Jesus suffered physical, emotional and mental pain during his life, and he died. Many other world religions find it inconceivable that God could have suffered pain and, yes, even died. Yet, Good Friday afternoon found him sharing the fate of all humanity. Because of Jesus, we need never believe that God abandons us in our pain, or on our deathbed. St. Paul wrote that no "trial, or distress, or persecution, or hunger . . . neither death nor life . . . will be able to separate us from the love of God that comes to us in Christ Jesus, our Lord" (Rom 8:35-39 NAB).

Resurrection and Incarnation

During his earthly ministry, Jesus revealed that God is with us in our poverty, our everyday responsibilities, our suffering, and in death. This is good news, indeed! For some reason, however, most of us expect more sensational signs from God. Even John the Baptist asked questions. After he was thrown in prison by Herod, John was undoubtedly kept abreast of what was happening with Jesus through reports from his own disciples. What he kept hearing confused him, though, and so he sent a few of his disciples to ask Jesus, "Are you 'He who is to come' or do we look for another?" Jesus replied by saying that his presence among the poor, the sick and the outcasts ought to be good news enough (Mt 11:2-6 NAB). This is a message we need to continue reflecting upon in this age when sensationalism is such an important diversion for our bored and restless society.

From the foregoing, it might appear that Jesus revealed a God who could care less for the rich and/or the healthy. Did he not, in fact, state that it would be difficult for the rich to enter the kingdom of heaven (Mk 10:23-27), and that the healthy did not need his doctoring (Mt 9:10-13)? His words concerning riches and health, however, should not be taken out of context. Some of his closest friends—Mary, Margaret and Lazarus—were apparently wealthy; Joseph of Arimathea and Nicodemus, two members of the religious ruling class, were also well off. There is no record of any of Jesus' disciples being sickly; more than likely, they were all strong, robust individuals, with stamina equal to the many hardships of the gospel trail. Jesus' words concerning the pitfalls of health and wealth only make sense in the context of his ministry to the human spirit. Material riches often give a false sense of self-sufficiency which robs us of the poverty of spirit that is a necessary prerequisite to experiencing a need for God. Physical and mental health—especially when it leads to self-righteousness—can also rob us of poverty of spirit if we forget the ultimate source of these very great gifts. But Jesus' example does not give us reason to over-romanticize poverty and categorically condemn wealth.

INCARNATION: GOD IS WITH US

He knew very well that many of the poor with whom he rubbed shoulders would be only too happy to attain wealth so as to use it for personal gain. The good news revealed by Jesus is that God does not withhold his presence from anyone on the basis of economics, physical looks, or level of intelligence.

With his resurrection into glory, the presence of God mediated through Jesus became immediately available to all people everywhere and in all times. No longer limited by the confines of space and time, Jesus is free now to become incarnate in our lives. "Exalted at God's right hand, he first received the promised Holy Spirit from the Father, then poured this Spirit out on us" (Acts 2:33 NAB). Faith means coming to believe that God can still come to us in our poverty, ordinariness, pain, suffering, riches and health because the same Jesus who once extended God's hands in these common situations is more able than ever to touch our lives.

God can do no more to communicate himself to all people without pre-empting our free will, which would negate any possibility of a real love relationship between ourselves and God. If we are waiting for a sign of God's presence in our world any more meaningful than what God has already revealed through Jesus Christ, then it may well be that we are looking for someone other than a God of love. In Jesus Christ, God has shared with us the deepest desires of his heart. The only thing left is for us to recognize our own poverty of spirit and receive the new life Christ brings to us in gratitude and joy. Then will the incarnation continue through us as we, in our own lives, continue the work of healing and reconciliation already begun by Jesus and continued in his risen person.

Three

New Life

It is obvious in the Acts of the Apostles, which probably comes as close as possible to capturing the spirit of the early church, that those who believed Jesus of Nazareth was raised to new life were beside themselves with joy. As we read through the Acts, however, and learn of the incredible sacrifices that believers made for the sake of the gospel, we might wonder about a couple of questions:

1. Why did the apostles believe that the resurrection had implications for their own destiny? Why was it not something for Jesus alone?

2. Why did they try to form communities? Why not just keep the message to themselves?

Had the apostles experienced no hope for resurrection themselves, Christianity would have been a very different movement. Jesus might have been acknowledged as a premier guru of some kind, his resurrection validating his teachings. Jesus' way to spiritual growth might have been proclaimed; converts would have been encouraged to embrace his way and, hence, grow into their own enlightenment—possibly even rise to new life themselves. But this kind of self-development program is not the proclamation we find in the New Testament.

Paul says very little about Jesus' teachings and refers even less to any spiritual methodology which the disciple might follow in order to attain salvation. Central to the proclamation of the "good news" was not Jesus' teachings, but Jesus himself, the crucified one who has risen to new life. The new life in Christ which the apostles invited others to experience was not something that could be earned as, for example, a jogger earns good health. The new life came to those who, through faith, opened themselves to relationship with the risen Christ. This new life was the Spirit of Jesus.

How did the apostles arrive at their proclamation rather than a program of self-salvation? Why was so much emphasis placed on relationship with Jesus? First of all, because this was what had changed the apostles' lives. Before they experienced the Spirit of the risen Christ they knew his teachings quite well, but were broken and impotent nonetheless. It was Jesus himself who transformed them into new men. Secondly, the apostles maintained that Jesus had commanded them to go forth and share this news, promising to be with them always. He also told them that he would raise to new life all who believed in him and would be in heaven preparing a place for all believers. The good news was the risen Jesus, the Lord who sought to become part of the lives of all people, leading humanity into the fullness of God's reign.

Compelled by a mandate they believed to have issued from the risen Christ, the apostles began proclaiming their perception of what had been the significance of the life, death and resurrection of Jesus. What followed were phenomena they probably could never have even fantasized in their wildest moments. One wonders whether they would have followed Jesus if they had, when hearing his call, comprehended all that would be entailed. In short, they founded a world religion and became simultaneously the most-loved and most-hated men in their area of the world. Their message went out ahead of them and followed them wherever they went; their reputation was undoubtedly as much a curse as a blessing. With one exception they all died martyrs, refusing to compromise their proclamation just as their Lord and master had refused to alter his own. But the movement did not end with their deaths. Long before even the first martyrs had shed their blood, it became apparent that the good news was contagious.

The Conversion Experience

What was experienced by those who heard the apostles preach? What did the early Christians believe about themselves? Finally, we are asking the kinds of questions that the New Testament addresses most often.

What we find is that the good news proclaimed by the apostles did indeed attract a sizeable number of people, although it was surely rejected by many. Since the message proclaimed by the apostles was very similar to that proclaimed by the church today, it is likely that those who heard them responded in as many and diverse ways as we do today. The only difference between then and now is that the apostles were much closer to their experience of Jesus and so they probably spoke with more conviction than do many of today's ministers. This difference could be quite significant, but we have no way of comparing.

Those who first heard the apostles must have found them extraordinarily assured in their values and faith convictions. Listeners must have noted a power and vitality emanating from them and sensed a response in their own feelings. This feeling resonated with the thoughts generated from a careful listening to the good news, and within a short period of time each listener had probably decided what was to be his or her response. Those who felt threatened by the message and vitality of the apostles and who did not care to invest the energy required to make changes in their lives probably jeered or else walked away. Some may have felt so threatened by this call to change that they were provoked to anger and even violence. The apostles allowed a mediocre spirit no neutral ground; they invited change and were perceived as threatening to the selfish and lazy spirits who heard them.

There were also those who were encouraged by what they heard and saw, of course. These were the people who were looking for a reason to hope, or else for a way to live more abundantly. Doubtlessly there were also those who found relief from the heavy burdens of guilt and anxiety they carried, as well as those hapless "broken wings" of society who always seem to gravitate to a caring community. The seed of the good news fell on various types of ground, as Jesus had predicted it would. Fortunately, there was much rich soil out in the world in the many good people who formed the earliest Christian communities.

What the early Christians experienced proved to be as transforming an encounter as the apostles' experience had been. Although they did not receive the same kind of manifestation of Jesus as had the apostles, those who believed on their words soon began to think, feel and act differently. Perhaps they felt God's presence in their lives more intimately, or at least in a special way when the community gathered to worship. Perhaps Christian spiritual discipline allowed them to better focus their life energies on tasks that were more consonant with human nature. Perhaps it was the enthusiasm of Christian fellowship, or perhaps all of the above that constituted the essence of the conversion experience. The explanation for the new life given by those who experienced it was that God had somehow become the animating center of their lives, and faith in Jesus had made this possible. *The same kinds of transformations are reported by Christians today*, although no one today has eaten grilled fish with the risen Jesus.

The Life in the Spirit

The New Testament explains that the transformation of a person takes place primarily in the mind and the spirit. In the mind, the vision of reality embraced by the Christian replaces a narrower, less-hopeful vision. The mind becomes freed from the shackles of guilt and anxiety which threaten to sabotage the best of our creative energies. We shall say more about the Christian vision of life later, but for now we must acknowledge its importance while admitting that Christian philosophy was of lesser significance to converts than the spiritual experience they participated in. The didactic message of Christianity has as much to say as does any philosophy of life, but in the long run one's intellectual vision of life counts for nought if one does not possess the power to live out that vision.

When Paul encountered those who proclaimed the gospel in only a didactic sort of manner, he challenged them to a deeper experience (see Acts 19:1–7). Christians believe they are blessed with the power to live out their vision of life by the Spirit of God working in their own spirits, nurturing the development of a new identity in Christ and providing motivation to follow Christ. This Holy Spirit is considered to be none other than the Spirit who had empowered Jesus during his earthly ministry and who was now poured out among believers with incredible generosity. In some way, this outpouring of the Spirit had been won by Jesus.

When we consider the new life in the Spirit, many of us think of people speaking in tongues, falling into trances, working miraculous healings, or prophesying in the name of God. While these phenomena are recorded in scripture and are evidenced in pentecostal communities today, they are not at the heart of the Christian experience of the Holy Spirit. At the heart of the pentecostal experience is an overflowing of love nurtured by the Trinitarian life of God. It is the extraordinary power of this love which enables Christians to build communities and to live out their vision of a life centered in Christ.

The resurrection of Jesus is believed by Christians to have won for humanity the opportunity to be deeply embraced by God in a new way. This is not to say that no experience of God was possible before Jesus rose from the dead; the Old Testament and the scriptures of all religions belie this proposition. The depth of intimacy with God experienced by Christians was not evidenced in many Jewish communities, however, where behavioral orientation according to the Law was stressed instead. The resurrection of Jesus established his complete oneness with God and made it possible for believers to enjoy the very life of God which Jesus himself enjoyed. In their deepest selves, Christians claimed to experience God filling them with love and power, launching them outward toward their brothers and sisters in Christ in love and appreciation unto the fullness of growth.

The Christian in community inevitably became aware of one of the most startling paradoxes of human nature: unity differentiates. Although it is true that involvement in a collective sometimes discourages individual development, this is not the case in healthy groups. The Christian in community, ever growing closer to other people and to God, does not lose his or her individuality in the body of Christ as does a drop of rain in the ocean. Unity differentiates: The closer one gets to another person in love and freedom, the more true to oneself one becomes. The human self is ultimately relational in nature, and the Christian in community has many opportunities to have mirrored back to him or her a variety of loving reflections which affirm the dignity of the self. The deeper the relationships one establishes in community, the more clearly does the mirror of other people reflect back who we are. Because of their relationships with one another in Christ, Christians have an excellent opportunity to discover who they are as individuals and how they may best serve God—each in his or her own way.

Four

The Mystical Body

As the early communities grew, Christians eventually came into identity themselves as the body of Christ on earth. Believing that the Spirit working in them was the Spirit which had empowered Jesus, it was inevitable that Christians would arrive at this insight.

Paul's conversion experience further emphasized the concept of the church as the body of Christ. "Saul, Saul, why do you persecute me?" asked Jesus on the road to Damascus. That Jesus so fully identified himself with his followers undoubtedly influenced Paul's theology of church.

The significance of this concept of church cannot be overstated. Because the followers of Jesus understood themselves to be essential and indispensable members of his Mystical Body, they shared a special and profound intimacy with one another. "See how those Christians love one another," reads one of the earliest references to the church by an outsider. Then, as now, this kind of loving fellowship filled many human needs.

Many people today lament the rise of organized religion. They believe that the loosely connected communities of the early church serve as an example of the social form that Christianity should have maintained. But heresies threatened even our utopian early church from within as well as without. Without the leadership of the apostles, the communities would have so dissipated and fragmented as to reduce the church to spiritual impotency. Thus it was that the early church organized itself along the lines discerned by apostolic authority. That this organization later became institutionalized as the official Roman state religion is another matter altogether.

When it became apparent that Jesus was not returning as soon as had been expected, and when the first generation witnesses began dying out, a method for transmitting the apostolic authority became crucial. Bishops became recognized as successors to the apostles, entrusted with the consensus teachings that had been discerned through the fires of persecution and heresy. The Mystical Body was no free-floating amoeba drifting along in a hostile world; the church was a community with authoritative leadership, direction and a sense of mission.

Toward the end of the first generation of Christianity it also became apparent that the understanding of Jesus and the church which had emerged ought to be written down. Curiously, we find very few writings from the early church other than the letters of Paul, although scripture scholars surmise the existence of writings on the sayings of Jesus predating any of the gospels. After 90 A.D. — well into the second generation of the church — Christian writings became more numerous. What is important for us to realize here is that the New Testament books came to us from the church. They were written by people in the church and expressed traditions already affirmed in the church. Furthermore, it was the church which confirmed the New Testament writings as inspired, rejecting certain writings as unfaithful to the consensus understanding ultimately rooted in apostolic authority. The reason why Christians so revere the New Testament is that it provides for all generations a lasting guide to the meaning of the life of Jesus and the early church.

Christian Identity

If the crucifixion of Jesus meant failure and devastation to his cause, resurrection signified the complete affirmation of his teachings, lifestyle and promises. It was with special care that the apostles explained to their communities what Jesus had said and what he had done in certain circumstances. While tradition had it that what could be written about Jesus would be impossible to contain in volumes of manuscripts, certain formulae to express the significance of his life and the salvific roles he embraced did emerge.

1. *Revealer*. He is the one who shows us what God is like and what a human being can be. He focuses in his person the two most urgent religious questions asked by the human mind: What kind of God is God, and what does God expect of human beings?

2. *Redeemer*. This role proceeds from the first. As the anointed of God who reveals God, Jesus was led

to a decisive confrontation with the forces of sin. He held fast to his resolve to do God's will and his trust in God's power to save, but was killed by the prevailing authorities of his day because of his convictions. By rising from the dead, however, Jesus conclusively broke the power of sin, opening a door through which the believer, too, might conquer sin and its wages, death.

    3. *Sanctifier*. Jesus' victory over sin and death and his exaltation at the right hand of God was followed by an outpouring of the Holy Spirit. This power, which is the power of God revealed in Jesus' resurrection, now became shared most generously with humanity.

After the communities gained some insight into Jesus' identity and his salvific roles, it was only natural that the church, his body in space and time, would perceive for itself similar roles. The church recognized its mission in the world to be three-fold: priestly, prophetic and kingly. The priestly role includes a mandate to minister and celebrate, especially in a liturgical context, the redemption which Jesus has won; the prophetic role emphasizes evangelization and teaching, a continuation of Jesus' role as revealer; the kingly role, modeled on the servant leadership of Jesus, is a call to serve other people. All of these roles, however, describe the responses of Christians whose primary motivation is the love of God. Attempts to describe and put on any or all of these roles are destined for failure or else a venture in self-conceit if not motivated by the love of God.

In summary, the resurrection of Jesus and the church which emerged in response offers three important experiences to church members. First of all, conversion itself enables individuals to sense more deeply the Spirit of God in their lives. The knowledge that one is loved by God in the depths of one's being—a knowledge which faith awakened—imparts perhaps the most powerful experience of meaning available to any human being. Secondly, the fellowship of other people in community brings support, friendship and a sense of identity. Because the groups to which we belong are so critical to our spiritual formation, belonging to and participating in Christian group life meets many very important human needs. Finally, authoritative leadership gives individuals in the church clear messages with which to struggle. The response of obedience invited by the bishops honors the dignity of individual judgment; it does not call for mindless submission. Paradoxically, individuals who decide to heed the word of God as discerned by the bishops realize depths of freedom and dignity they never dreamed possible.

Five

When Good Things Happen to Bad People

    A prevailing myth adopted by many today has it that good, clean living will bring health, prosperity and the respect of others. The origins of this myth probably derive from much of life experience, for there is considerable data in support of this assumption. If nothing else, modern psychology has taught us that our actions, thoughts and feelings are all related. It follows that healthy thinking and clean living go hand in hand. This myth might also be, in part, an expression of our own hope that efforts to live ethically will be rewarded. Very often it is much more difficult to be honest, responsible and charitable than to be crooked, lazy and selfish, and we all hope that our effort to do what is right won't go unrewarded.

The Old Testmant very often seems to be in complete accord with what we shall call the Prosperity Myth. God's promises are couched in terms of prosperity, the patriarchs are held out as models of the good life, and we are guaranteed that obedience to the Law will bring long days and full living. The fact that Jews sustained this belief for thousands of years is additional evidence of the credibility of the Prosperity Myth, for orthodox Jews did not hope for a heavenly life after death. Had the myth gone completely against the grain of life experiences, Judaism would have been a different religion with different hopes and beliefs.

As we all know, however, the Prosperity Myth does not speak to the totality of life experiences; in fact, it ignores many disturbing problems. What about those born with physical or mental defects? What about those who work hard and live clean but seem never to find their way out of poverty and misfortune? What about debilitating sicknesses that strike people in the prime of their lives? Although healthy-mindedness can reduce susceptibility to many illnesses, we are never completely invulnerable to some kind of virus or accident. Then there is death! Does the Prosperity Myth remain relevant in the face of death? Is the thought that we shall leave the world a better place because of our children and our work completely consoling? Finally, the most serious challenge to the Prosperity Myth comes from those who prosper, but who live evil lives and experience few adverse consequences in this life.

Jews were aware of all these challenges to the Prosperity Myth and they faced each one bravely, attempting to explain how it might be properly understood. Sickness, suffering and death were problems, to be sure, but were these not part of the punishment we brought on ourselves as a consquence of the fall in Eden? Rather than curse God for suffering, the faithful Jew might have instead thanked God that things were not worse. If a good person suffered or failed to achieve prosperity, this was an injustice, but very often the Jews regarded suffering as a tool used by God to bring about repentance and reconciliation. Suffering did not necessarily negate all avenues for hope.

Death was another matter. No possibility for reincarnation was entertained, and not until Greek influences gave rise to Hellenistic Judaism in about the fourth century B.C. did Jews hope for full living in an afterlife. The dead went to Sheol, a realm of shadows and inactivity. If this all seems a poor metaphysical system—one deeply riddled with existential holes—just remember that it has worked for almost 4,000 years. Life itself to a Jew was considered a great, unearned blessing; one simply had to take the bad with the good.

Jewish thinkers had extreme difficulty reconciling the prosperity of the wicked with the justice of God, however. The initial hope that the unjust would receive their recompense in this life proved time after time in generation after generation to be unrealized. "I would like to debate a point of justice with you," Jeremiah boldly challenged God (Jer 12, 1-3 JB). "Why is it that the wicked live so prosperously? Why do scoundrels enjoy peace? You plant them, they take root, and flourish, and even bear fruit. . . . Drag them off like sheep for the slaughter-house," he pleads in behalf of the Prosperity Myth.

Earlier in Jewish history, the Psalmist had raised the same questions in Psalm 94, going further than Jeremiah by pointing out that some of these people were quite arrogant in their wickedness, "boasting and asserting themselves . . . murdering and massacring widows, orphans and guests." The Psalmist reconciled this injustice by believing that "God will pay them back for all their sins, and will silence their wickedness." Fine words, but when, might we ask, will God pay them back for their sins? The wicked continue to prosper generation after generation, suffering occasional setbacks, but always seeming to recover and entrench themselves more deeply in human history. They still, to this very day, generate terrorism for the express purpose of disrupting social order; they murder the innocent; they oppress the poor; they deprive human beings of the freedoms written into the laws of our nature. Most of them get away with it unpunished, causing us to ask if our hope for justice is not completely unrealistic in the first place.

The Challenge of Job

Nowhere have questions concerning the justice of God been focused and discussed more comprehensively than in the Old Testament Book of Job. A literary masterpiece, the work portrays a good and holy man, Job, nonetheless suffering infirmity and the complete loss of what had once been a prosperous business and a large, healthy family. Job has no control over this situation; he could have done nothing to prevent it.

Initially, he rises to the occasion, blessing God who has given, but now has chosen to take away; eventually, he beings lamenting the day he was born and everything which followed thereafter. The appearance of a few friends to accuse him of sin is no consolation at all, only convincing Job even more so of his innocence and of the inadequacy of the Prosperity Myth. Job's friends assume the role as defendants of the Prosperity Myth, insisting that he must have offended God in some manner or else he would not be suffering as he is. Even his wife hounds him to lay bare his hidden sin, that her life, too, might be restored to its former happiness.

Suffering so intensely that he can scarcely think at all, Job resists the accusations of wife and friends, holding God alone responsible for what had happened to him, ever careful to acknowledge God's right to do as he pleases with his creatures. Job notes, however, the contrast between his situation and the prosperity of the wicked, wondering aloud what this says about the justice of God. "If God wants people to show up the wicked with good example and charity, then why has God punished a just and holy man like me?" Job queries. God is thus challenged to explain himself or else suffer an embarrassing setback insofar as respect for his justice and mercy is concerned.

Reading through chapters 38–42, we might, with Job, feel overwhelmed by the power of God and the irrelevancy of his response. The closest he comes to replying to Job's questions is, "Do you really want to reverse my judgment, and put me in the wrong to put yourself in the right?" There is not even a remote semblance of ethical principle in this statement; God is begging the question, at best. Another boasting of his power follows, all of which reduces Job to a state of humble impotence; he lays his hand over his mouth, refusing to say more. God then restores Job to health and prosperity, thus reinstating himself as the all-powerful judge and rewarder of the good.

While the Book of Job provides us with an exhaustive reflection on the nature of evil and the justice of God, its conclusions leave much unsaid. Certainly, we can appreciate the restoration of Job's health and prosperity, but there are millions living today who have not experienced such restitution and will never do so in this world. Also, we have learned nothing new about God's response to the prosperity of the wicked except that he knows all about it and has lots of power to do something about it if he so decides.

Christianity and Justice

It is against the backdrop of Job's challenge that we can best appreciate the significance of the resurrection of Jesus toward advancing the cause of God's justice. The church interpreted the resurrection to demonstrate the existence of life after death. Furthermore, Jesus taught that God will judge all people on the basis of the kind of life they have lived; the good will receive the reward they have already begun to experience in their lives; and the evil will be allowed to experience the fullness of the misery they have brought upon others and written into their own being. In a sense, the Prosperity Myth is vindicated by the resurrection, so long as its promises are extended from this life into the hereafter.

No one is completely good or bad, as we know, and the simplistic model of judgment described in the gospels raises many questions about those areas of grey in all our lives. This is not the place for reflection on such issues, however. Nor are we interested, here, in speculating on whether or not God's judgment is perceived at the moment of death or in some later period with all of humanity present. We do want to note the implication that there is something in all of us that is immoral, and which will, after death, be without any of the props and supports which keep us distanced from God during our time on earth. Distinguishing between the good and the bad among us will be God's task, and he will minister justice in wisdom and equity.

Had Job known of the resurrection, he might have borne his sufferings more patiently. Had he known of the risen Jesus who had previously been the crucified Jesus—tortured in innocence just as he had been—Job might have dismissed his self-righteous friends in complete peace of mind. The justice Job hungered for was finally assured in the resurrection. The significance of this belief to the individual and societies can hardly be exaggerated.

For the individual, the prospect of immortality and judgment is a sobering thought. Only an atheist, it would seem, could shake free from the ethical imperatives which follow from this perspective. Confronted with the possibility of an eventual call to accountability, the individual is challenged to a purity of behavior allowing for none of the usual rationalizations of the unethical. "Everybody does it," and "It's OK so long as you don't get caught" are seen now as empty slogans. You will get caught, Christianity promises, and if everybody has been unethical, then everybody will get caught. *The product of judgment is a call to live before God rather than in comparison with others*, aligning our behavior with the causes of God rather than with mere cultural whims and fads. There can be little doubt that this Christian doctrine of judgment has helped to make people a little more honest and better-behaved then they would otherwise have been compelled to be.

From the foregoing, it might seem that judgment works only as a negative reinforcement—sort of like the threat of a spanking with small children. This is only half of the doctrine, however. Certainly, the fear of eternal punishment generated by the prospect of judgment has been exploited by ministers through the ages, but many people are not scared by this anymore. As Lawrence Kohlberg has demonstrated in his research, the fear of punishment is a very primitive level of moral development. It is comforting to know that Christianity can address people at such a basic level of morality, but there is much on the positive side of morality for those who have moved along in their growth in moral awareness.

God's judgment, we might recognize, is not an act which God bestows for or against us; rather, judgment is determined in our own response to God. Our earthly life is, in this perspective, an opportunity to write in the law of our being the values of God or the values of self-indulgence. When, at the end of our days, we stand before God stripped of all our defense mechanisms and false pretenses, we will either be drawn toward him or else feel repulsed by his love. It is not so much that God will reject those who have been evil; it is they who will not be able to accept God in his revealed splendor. Like feeble seedlings in highly fertilized soil, they will be shriveled up, their hardened hearts closed to the power of the Love that reaches out to embrace them. Those who have loved God and their fellow human beings, on the other hand, will have become acclimated, as it were, to the richness of the Divine Ground. They will burst forth in a passionate embrace of the God who has embraced them through their lives, nurturing them unto the fullness of their spiritual individuality.

The Christian doctrine of judgment stresses the importance of the small decisions we make in addition to the very few large ones we struggle with from time to time. "Those who are great in the little things will be great in the larger things," said Jesus. "If you want to know what you think of God and his cause, look at the decisions you make every day and, especially, the criteria you employ when making them," counsels Christian morality. We write the law of our being through the small decisions we make each day. That our decisions can assume eternal significance is a uniquely Christian contribution, stemming from reflection on the meaning of the resurrection of Jesus. The dignity thus conferred on decision-making, a distinctly human activity, should pervade the life of anyone who takes the prospect of divine judgment seriously. This is the positive side of the doctrine of judgment, an emphasis which has the potential of conferring meaning on even the most mundane of decisions we make each day.

Six

Courage to Live

If the resurrection of Jesus had propagated only the church and the promise of judgment, it would, on those merits alone, deserve our most serious consideration. Yet, the critic looking for reasons to ignore Jesus' invitation to new life could develop a rationale for turning away. He or she might maintain that Christianity is but an escapist, otherworldly religion, its followers intoxicated with "too much heaven on their minds," as the Judas of *Jesus Christ, Superstar* complained. The threat of eternal damnation could be called a cheap scare tactic, at worst an oppressive means utilized by church leaders to coerce people into supporting them.

These arguments probably sound familiar to the reader who has tried at one time or another to explain what Christianity is about to a person who is close-minded and filled with self-justifications. But as the previous chapters have explained, belonging to Christian community and belief in the eventuality of judgment do not necessarily translate into a fear-based fellowship. Church and judgment are by no means the only significant existential factors gained by the resurrection.

To the Christian who takes the resurrection of Jesus to be truth, there is potential for an ever-deepening realization of the lifting of a terrible constraint on human growth: anxiety caused by the fear of death.

Fear of Death

Death, wrote William James, is the worm in the core of the apple of life. Awareness of the inevitability of death is possible because we, as conscious beings, possess the ability to project ourselves into the future; we do not, like simpler animals, live only instinctively in the present moment. Knowing that we shall die is one of our most uniquely human characteristics.

All around us we see death. Plants sprout, bear seed, then die; birds lay eggs, hatch their young, the nestlings grow up to raise their own young, then they too die; pets die, distant acquaintances die, relatives die, and deeply loved ones die. We know that this same law of life applies to us, too, but death is such an unpleasant reality to face that we usually build up a myriad of defenses to prevent ourselves from facing the implications of our own mortality. If you do not believe this, note your reaction the next time you read in the paper or hear a report of an auto accident in which some previously healthy person was killed. "Too bad, but I'm more careful," we typically respond. "Couldn't happen to me," we lie to ourselves. Notice in that moment the sense of unreality accompanying your thoughts about the death of this unfortunate. The deaths of hundreds or even thousands of people leave us even more disaffected. The worm in the core of the apple of life is not a pleasant reality to face.

The fear of death shows up in our lives in a number of ways. It contributes in part to our seemingly insatiable desire to avoid aging and accounts for much of the insecurity we feel when we consider the future. It generates concern about future economic markets, insurance and wills of testament. In his Pulitzer Prize-winning book, *The Denial of Death*, Ernest Becker shows how awareness of our mortality is a significant factor in the development of our most basic levels of personality. In addition, we today are the first generation in history who suffer the dubious honor of struggling with the prospect of nuclear holocaust and the total death it would bring—an immense destruction perhaps annihilating the continuity of human progress thus far achieved. Who among us can think of the possibility of life on earth 50 years into the future without secretly doubting that there will be a planet worth living on when that time comes? Anxieties, worries and insecurities ultimately rooted in the fear of death cloud many of our most positive experiences and shape the margins of our lifestyle. Playing it extra safe in life, which the fear of death encourages, deprives us of many potentially worthwhile experiences. Despairing of life, which death also influences, leads many people to suicide or else tuning out of life in some form of escape.

While the fear of death might be a natural, instinctive adaptation, there is no doubt that this instinctual level of awareness is also nourished by our thoughts about death. Death means at least the complete cessation of life as we know it. Even belief in a glorious afterlife of some sort does not completely remove this fear. Death means change of the most drastic, uncontrollable kind, and there is a basic conservatism in all of us which resists change. For those who do not believe in life after death, thoughts about death might bring a terror far worse than a primal resistance to change. Those who lack any basis for hoping in a survival of the mind and spirit usually encounter deep within themselves a severe case of doubt as to the meaning of life. Death, for the hopeless, means not change, but self-obliteration, the ultimate in existential absurdities. Undoubtedly, this fear of self-obliteration is present to some extent in even the most ardent Christian.

Coping With Death

There is a certain amount of consolation to be derived from reflection on the fact that death is a universal phenomenon. Much of our resistance to death springs from the feeling that we shall thereafter be left out of the ongoing march of life through history. Realizing that everyone will have to face death leaves us feeling less alone, and helps us to commit ourselves to making our own marks in time. The theory of evolution also suggests that the death of older individuals is necessary for making room on this earth for the next generation. Because we have offspring, we must die so that they and their offspring might not be crowded out. Death, in this perspective, might be viewed as an act of love for future generations.

It is doubtful that many people are much consoled by the thoughts above, however. What about those who have no children? How can they rationalize death as being necessary for their children's sake? And what about our sense of personal identity? Isn't that what really makes the thought of death so unalterably absurd? Are we merely bricks upon which future generations may add more bricks as humanity builds its home upon the earth? Certainly this offers little consolation to our innate egoism!

The resurrection of Jesus casts a new light on the meaning of death and dying. *Death means not only making way for the next generation, but continuing our own personal journey in growth.* Dying does not signify the imminence of self-obliteration, but the birthing of an individual into new life. Personal identity survives in God's Spirit because God is a living God and whatever God loves will live in God's life, which is eternal. Unlike any other religion or philosophy, Christianity affirms the dignity of the individual human life.

For those of us who must watch our loved ones die, the resurrection of Jesus promises that our separation from them is only temporary. Going on without loved ones will be difficult, but we do so knowing that our own continuing growth in this life will bring us together with them in the next life. Because they have died, we must now commit ourselves to living more fully in love.

Belief in the resurrection can go quite far in helping us overcome our fear of death. We must not stop at that point, however. The prospect of our own individual resurrection should make us bold in living life in the here and now. The reticence and mediocrity spawned by the fear of death must be swept away now, for there is really nothing to be afraid of. If we really believe in the resurrection, we must become more willing to lay down our lives for the sake of love, truth and justice in this world now.

Christians who have made a committed effort to

live close to Christ actually claim to experience an ever-deepening intimacy with God throughout the years. Their belief in life after death and a fuller life in Christ becomes a conviction so strong as to dispel almost completely all fear and insecurity from their hearts. Gradually, death might even be anticipated, the joys of heaven bringing consolation even in this life. For the Christian, the resurrection of Jesus shows that nothing—not even death—can separate the believer from the love of God.

Seven

The Meaning of Suffering

Belief in the resurrection of Jesus should help to diminish anxiety toward the future brought on by the fear of death. For healthy people, this might be an almost completely liberating experience, freeing them to experience life more fully in the here and now. Many others, however, are weighed under by tremendous burdens of guilt, shame and physical suffering. Most of us, at some time during our lives, experience these pains to a great degree. When this happens, learning to cope with pain becomes a critical task.

One of the world's greatest religious thinkers, Gautama Buddha, stated as the first of his Four Noble Truths that "Life is suffering." He then went on to point out that suffering is caused by selfish craving and outlines an eightfold path of moderation to diminish suffering. Buddha's way called for a gradual obliteration of ego-craving, which, in turn, led to a reduction in the experience of pain. Nirvana, the ultimate in spiritual experiences for the Buddhist, is described as a complete absence of a sense of ego and, hence, pain.

The Christian attitude toward suffering is entirely different. If there were Noble Truth corollaries to Buddhism in Christian dogma, the first would undoubtedly be that "Life is good." This is what God says about creation in Genesis 1, so it is the starting point for thinkers in the Judeo-Christian tradition who struggle with the meaning of life. Furthermore, the resurrection of Jesus points up the dignity of the individual while his crucifixion suggests that there is a connection between suffering and new life experiences. How are we to make sense out of all of this?

Kinds of Suffering

It might be helpful in beginning a discussion on the meaning of suffering to differentiate between various experiences of pain. For our purposes, let us recognize four basic sources of pain.

1. *Growth pains* are imposed upon us from without and within by the imperative to change. Because change usually requires that we stretch our physical, mental and emotional boundaries, there is pain associated with change. Our movements from infancy through childhood, adolescence, adulthood, the middle years and old age and death are inescapably accompanied by suffering. This suffering might be minimized through the care of loving friends and family members, but it cannot be avoided altogether.

2. *Self-induced pain* results from behaviors that we ourselves initiate out of ignorance or even consciousness, but which hurt us in some way. Guilt and shame are two common experiences of self-induced pain, usually resulting from behaviors that go against our values. Lung cancer caused by smoking cigarettes, heart problems resulting from overeating and accidents because of negligence are other examples of suffering that can be prevented to some extent if we are willing to make certain lifestyle adjustments.

3. *Social shortfall pains* are caused by inadequacies in our systems of government, communications and economics. Wars, famines and certain epidemics are preventable in the sense that we often know of remedies to avoid them, but fail to do so. Individuals experiencing pain because of social shortcomings usually experience their misfortunes as unavoidable; there is little that they could do to prevent the problem, but there would have been a way to avoid the tragedy if government had been prepared.

4. *Accidental pain* is unavoidable and tragic. Birth defects, floods, earthquakes and many forms of sickness and accidents are all seemingly impossible to predict or prevent. These are events which leave us asking, "Why me, Lord?" Often there is no completely satisfactory answer except to attribute the tragedy to bad luck. For the religious person, this time can tax faith to the extremes.

Many of our experiences of suffering involve a combination of the above. Consider divorce, for example. In the case of a young couple, they might realize that they married too young and have "grown apart" as they matured. The pains of divorce would thus be self-induced in that it is the result of poor choices made, but hopefully growing pains will also be pointing the way to a better future for both individuals. Perhaps a divorce might also follow some kind of an accident or social crisis, which strained an already tenuous relationship to the breaking point.

Regardless of the source of our pain, the important religious questions have to do with our attitude toward our experiences of suffering. Let us look at two opposing attitudes.

1. *Redemptive suffering* is pain borne with love in hope. People struggling in this manner grow deeper in their experiences of selfhood and in compassion for others. Once (or if) the time of struggle passes, these people can look back on the whole ordeal and be grateful that it has so helped them to grow to be more fully human.

2. *Unredemptive suffering* is characterized by anger and hopelessness, usually resulting from the absence of a sense of the meaning of the pains borne. People experiencing unredemptive or meaningless (to them) suffering do not grow through the ordeal. At the very worst, they become broken and indifferent and try to escape from life in some way.

Viktor Frankl, a survivor of the German concentration camps, wrote that it is possible to experience redemptive suffering in even the most oppressive situations. The critical question, therefore, seems to be how we can comprehend a sense of meaning during times of stress and struggle. It is with regard to this question that Christianity offers some of its most unique teachings.

The Meaning of Suffering

Christianity and Suffering

Salvaging a sense of the meaning of life's pains is one of the most important tasks of religion. Unfortunately, certain theologies move people away from God during their hard times. Consider, for example, some of the platitudes that we often use to console a suffering loved one.

1. "God is testing you in order to strengthen you."
2. "God would not have sent this if he thought you could not bear it."
3. "It doesn't make sense now, but one day you will look back and see God's reasons for all of this pain."
4. "The Lord works in strange ways."
5. (Regarding a tragic death.) "When the Lord pulls your number, your time is up."

The list could go on, but you get the idea. We use these statements to offer consolation, but their assumptions and implications are anything but reassuring. They all accept as a starting premise a belief that God has somehow caused or willed our misfortunes (or else he could have prevented them, but didn't). If this is indeed the case—as most people believe it is—then why should anyone feel compelled to turn for help to the very source of their pain? The statements above and the theologies implicit in them have caused untold numbers of people to abandon God when they needed him most.

There is nothing in the New Testament to support the notion that God is directly responsible for human suffering. On the contrary, if we believe that the resurrection validated Jesus' revelation of God, then we meet a deity interested in alleviating suffering in every way possible. Jesus never refused a request for healing, and never implicated God in any way with human misery. Suffering, to Jesus, was a fact of life to contend with; the real issue for Jesus concerned alleviating suffering, not explaining what it was.

For people suffering from growing pains, Jesus offers hope through his revelation that life is worth living. Growth through the years is not an absurd vanity, but an exciting adventure. Children must learn to walk and think, adolescents must find themselves, adults must learn to be responsible, intimate and generous, the elderly must accept the imminence of death gracefully. Life is not a gigantic universal accident, but a wonderful blessing. Life is good, and growth is an essential part of life.

People suffering from self-induced pains have a real friend in Jesus. To those who are laden by guilt and shame, he says, "Arise! Forget the past, and begin loving now and into the future. It's never too late to begin anew. Don't look back; your sins are forgiven, so forgive yourself and move on." If we need strength to make lifestyle adjustments to reduce stress, overeating and compulsive behaviors, we need only ask for grace and then begin attempting to change, knowing that we shall be given the strength to break free from self-destructive behaviors.

Jesus wills that we eventually eliminate all social shortfalls from our world. His weapons against this pervasive source of pain include knowledge, charity and spiritual power. He would have us understand ourselves and the world in which we live that we might better choose the manner in which we care for our bodies, manage the environment and govern our societies. This knowledge is to be governed by charity, which means that we ought to balance egoism with altruism. Because this challenge moves against the grain of our innate tendency toward selfish laziness, he gives us his Spirit to empower us along the way.

Accidental pain confronted Jesus at every turn, and it was here that he differed radically in his theology from his Jewish contemporaries. Most Jews did not distinguish between primary and secondary causality. God, to them, was directly involved in the opening of a flower, the conception of a child, the changing weather, sickness and death. But Jesus flatly denied that blindness was caused by God, that a falling tower was willed by God and that Pilate's moody persecutions were of God (Lk 13:1–9). Although a Jew, Jesus undoubtedly recognized the reality of bad luck and unfortunate tragedy. By thus "taking God off the hook" insofar as accidental pain is concerned, he prevented the building of walls of blame between the oppressed and God.

Jesus' attitude toward all forms of suffering—even the most blatant self-induced forms—was compassion. He realized that perhaps the hardest thing about suffering is going it alone. It is true that we must each bear our own pains bravely, but the support of others can help to diminish pain and give us perspective. Knowing that others have suffered even as we suffer keeps us from despairing and connects us with the larger human family.

No matter how unfair we believe our pains to be, no one of us will ever suffer more unjustly than did Jesus. In him, we encounter a God who has accepted the human condition completely, even to the point of suffering and dying as we do. His is a God we can turn to during all our experiences of pain, knowing that God understands our predicaments since Jesus has suffered with us. Furthermore, the resurrection of Jesus demonstrates that suffering borne in hope and love will bring us to new vistas of consciousness and joy. The risen Jesus was first the crucified Jesus, and we, too, will find this pattern repeating itself in our own lives if we can manage to turn our pains into redemptive suffering. The consolation of Christ we extend to one another during those times is one of the most important functions of our life in the church.

Eight

Meaning in Life

There comes a time in adult life when it seems as though growth slows down dramatically. We begin to believe that we know as much about people as there is to know, that we understand the way the world works and that we know what life is all about. The fallacy of this position is obvious, but the experience of ennui is far too common to brush off flippantly as mere shortsightedness. "Most people lead lives of quiet desperation," wrote Thoreau, and the author of the Book of Ecclesiastes seemed even more pessimistic. "Vanity of vanities; all is vanity!" wrote Qoheleth. "All things are wearisome. . . . What was will be again; what has been done will be done again; and there is nothing new under the sun" (Eccl 1:2,8,9 JB). In short, we are talking about the loss of interest in life, usually caused by the absence of a sense of meaning, or something to grow into.

In earlier days, the problem of loss of interest in life—of boredom—was not evidenced on so massive a scale as today. The struggle simply to survive created a sense of something to grow into (except in oppressive situations where the hope of betterment was negated). In the United States as recently as 40 years ago, the majority of people experienced this struggle simply to eat and find shelter. Notions about assuming a significant role in society were a luxury for the wealthy who had already been assured the basics in life. Today, however, the American social welfare state and a productive economy assures employment and the means of survival for an overwhelming majority of our people. With survival no longer an issue for so many of us, the quest for identity, meaning and significant work—self-actualization, as Maslow put it—has risen to the forefront as the great human challenge of our age.

Something to Grow Into

There have been, through the years, many approaches addressing the issue of personal growth. For Qoheleth, the answer was to be found in lowering expectations and contenting self with simple pleasures and good work (Eccl 2:24). Buddha's solution emphasized a systematic destruction of the ego and its desires, reducing personal identity to a state of blissful nothingness. On the other hand, Abraham Maslow described the self-actualizing person as one who is ambitious for growth and is involved in tasks which express some universal principle. In contrast with Buddha's passionless mystics, self-actualizing people evidence a strong sense of identity and personality; in contrast with Qoheleth's Jewish hedonists, they expect far more from life than simple pleasure and good work.

Maslow's studies of healthy people have affirmed, if nothing else, the inherent motivating power of universal values. An individual caught up in the pursuit of, say, justice might find meaning in life as a servant of justice—lawyer, police officer, activist, judge. Growth comes as the individual risks more and more in response to the demands of justice, enabling an ever-deepening internalization of the principles of justice. In time, the individual might even feel that he or she has become an incarnation of justice. If the self-actualizing person is drawn by several universal principles simultaneously, all will be incarnated to a greater or lesser degree. The problem of boredom and the absence of a sense of something to grow into seems to be a small problem for these people. The principles themselves act as motivators, calling them forth into virtually limitless dimensions of personal growth.

The Christian approach to personal growth is much more like that evidenced by Maslow's self-actualizing people than like Buddha's or Qoheleth's models. *Christian growth is a process emphasizing not self-immolation, but self-expansion into an ever-widening embrace of all creation and the God who creates.* Jesus is affirmed as the incarnation of all universal principles, calling the individual forward in a lifelong adventure of personal growth. In Jesus, universal principles become focused and personalized. Modeling the self on Jesus enables the Christian to incarnate truth, justice, honesty, love and all the other universal principles valued by self-actualizing people. But Christianity takes the process a step further than secular humanism, modeling the self in the person of Jesus Christ, who still lives to help us along.

Christian Meaning

It is tremendously edifying to note the manner in which universal principles mold human behavior. Even when severed from a specifically religious context, love, beauty, truth and justice hold an attraction that has ennobled many a person for living by their demands. Unfortunately, the abstract nature of these principles leaves them open to a wide range of interpretation.

"What *is* truth?" Pilate asked Jesus. Philosophers through the ages have wondered the same. And what in the world do we mean by love? Did Marx outline the shape of the just society, or did Adam Smith and Plato? Is beauty merely "in the eyes of the beholder"? What do we mean by truth, love, justice and beauty?

In Jesus Christ, universal principles become focused and defined more clearly. In him, beauty, truth, love and justice take on a new meaning. If we believe that the resurrection signifies God's affirmation of Jesus' life and teaching, we would do well to consider his values for living.

Love, for Jesus, meant the giving of one's self in order to facilitate the growth of another (and yourself as well in the process). This requires a putting to death of our selfish tendency to involve ourselves with others only insofar as it is convenient and/or beneficial to us. Christian love is a commitment we make to ourselves and others to give of ourselves for the sake of growth; this is how God loves us. "We love because God loved us first," wrote St. John. As we persevere in the Christian life, we eventually begin to love because we have become lovers.

Truth for the Christian includes not only what human reason and experience can validate, but also what God has revealed. Human reason is limited by space and time; revelation satisfies our deepest yearnings to comprehend the meaning of life, creation and death. Without revelation, we should be forever attempting to choose the truths about life from the myriad of philosophies articulated through history by sincere and painstaking philosophers. The resurrection of Jesus figures significantly here, elevating his teachings and those of the church to a height of credibility deserving at least as much attention as is given to worldly thinkers.

Justice, as we have noted in an earlier chapter, means that each individual human will eventually have to answer to God for his or her behavior. This does not mean that Christians ought to abandon the quest for justice in this life, however. Justice requires that we speak the truth in love for the sake of the oppressed, always conscious that the judgment of God is more than balanced by his mercy. So must it be for us.

Beauty, whatever it is, can be best apprehended by those who are pure of heart and free from anxiety and self-concern. Living a life of Christian love and reflecting on Christian truth enables us to perceive more beauty in ourselves and the world around us.

The follower of Jesus has much to live for. Life, for this person, can be charged with meaning at every turn. Opportunities to extend love, each in a unique way according to the talents possessed, present themselves many times each day. Truth is seemingly inexhaustible in its richness. The demands of justice are greater than ever before, calling for eager servants to stand with the oppressed. A world of beauty awaits the appreciative. Personal growth in these and other areas may be experienced all through life. There is no reason at all ever to become bored with life, for the adventure of growing in Christ is never completely finished.

Nine

The Reign of God

Sooner or later we all wonder about where we are headed as a community, nation, world. Because there is no centralized government directing and charting the directions of global development, we are bound to question whether or not the seemingly random patterns of growth observed in the varieties of nations will piece themselves together in such a way as to perpetuate creative progress, or whether the nations are destined eventually to clash and bring the world to oblivion. Is progress to a higher standard of material wellbeing with accompanying improvements in respect for human rights a realistic expectation? Where is history going?

Two philosophical views of history predominate, and they might, for the sake of convenience, be considered the Eastern and Western views. In the Eastern view, which was evidenced until recently in India, China and Japan, history is thought to move in a circular pattern. What lives finally dies and undergoes decay, the process then repeating; what we build shall ultimately count for nought. The only way to break out of this fatalistic cycle is to achieve complete unity with Being by putting to death the ego and all its desires.

A linear view of history predominates in the West. What lives is observed to die, but the elements of decay are recycled and utilized by other organisms; life evolves, ever building more complex forms out of simpler ones. There is no need to escape from the world, for the world is moving forward, and human beings have been entrusted with the role of engineering the movement. There are regressions, to be sure, but the spiral of history advances in ever tighter rings toward full humanization. The possibility of real progress is affirmed. This view of history predominates in capitalistic and Marxist nations.

The Eastern view of history derives from Hinduism, Buddhism, Taoism and Confucianism to some extent. The Western view is based primarily on the Judeo-Christian tradition. In the Eastern view, community formation and social justice are undetermined by an individualistic emphasis on salvation and a belief in reincarnation. If one has it bad now, then maybe there will be rebirth into more fortunate circumstances later. In the Western view, reincarnation is seldom admitted. Community networking is recognized to be essential for maximizing human potential, and social justice is a high priority.

The implications of either view of history are many as far as motivating behavior and community involvement are concerned. The industrial revolution and all that followed in medical technology, mass communication, population growth and a sense of global interdependence built upon the philosophical view of the West. As the West scurried along, flirting simultaneously with a golden age of prosperity and complete annihilation of the environment, Easterners sat passively by, many of them seeking to withdraw completely from the world of ordinary human activities. "Westerners are attempting a noble endeavor," an Easterner might concede, "but the circle will close." The recent surge of popularity enjoyed by Eastern religious movements in the West may well signify a growing pessimism toward Western prosperity myths.

Christianity and Progress

Although the church preached about Jesus, Jesus preached about the reign of God. To Jesus, the reign of God is to be characterized by justice, truth, peace and prosperity, all resulting from lives spent in love; it is the visible manifestation of the life of God among people. He taught his followers to pray that this kingdom might come on earth as it is already present in heaven, but added that it would emerge gradually only as a consequence of the reconciliatory leavening which Christians will exert in the world. The reign of God is already in our midst, yet it must be won through loving service if it is to become fully manifest among us.

The early church recognized in Jesus a full incarnation of the reign of God. When the church began proclaiming the good news, encouraging people to faith in Jesus, there was therefore no neglect of the message which Jesus had believed to be most important. Because the reign of God was already present and operative in the person of the risen Jesus, relationship with him and following in his way became, in essence, the fulfillment of the message which Jesus had preached. Jesus' body on earth, the church, assumed the role of harbinger of the reign of God, acting as a leaven of love in the world through time.

Because of the resurrection, Christians believe that the ultimate victory of the reign of God is guaranteed. The enemies of God's reign failed to thwart the designs of God when they crucified Jesus; the cornerstone which Jesus laid in human history will, therefore, withstand the tempests of time. Furthermore, the church stands on the promise of Jesus that the Holy Spirit will lead it into the fullness of truth, and that the gates of hell shall not prevail against it. Real progress for goodness and truth is assured. These are beliefs which we, who live in the shadow of nuclear devastation, need to claim if we are to remain sane.

The church's understanding of the reign of God is attractive on paper, but is there really any evidence that the world is moving toward greater justice, peace and prosperity? With nuclear weapons incubating in silos, with holocausts and genocide still fresh in our memories, with terrorism plaguing many countries and with gross violations of human rights taking place on a massive scale, where, might we ask, is the evidence for real progress toward goodness in the world?

The kind of objection raised above fails to consider the basis for Christian hope and optimism. Christianity is the religion of the individual, albeit in a community context. Christians recognize the fact that individuals can and do change (if they want to), becoming more loving and less destructive influences in society. And what, after all, are societies if not collections of individuals? If individuals can change, societies can change. That there is still blatant evidence of evil in the world is obvious, but centuries of laziness and malice cannot be leavened out quickly. Social structures must change to make way for the new wine of spiritual freedom given to us by the Holy Spirit, and structures do not change easily.

If one tries to evaluate the progress of the reign of God on a global scale, the results are sure to be confusing at this stage in history. Pockets of progress can be readily observed in subglobal units, however. Any vibrant Christian community includes inspiring examples of individual transformations; many also show growth in wisdom and intimacy through the years. On a larger scale, the church, in spite of all its lingering problems, has certainly matured in its knowledge of and commitment to the coming of the reign of God. Perhaps it is stretching things a bit to say that many Western countries are becoming more humanized, but several encouraging signs can be noted. In the United States, for example, our respect for human rights for previously oppressed groups has slowly and gradually been upheld. We have, during the past century, witnessed the elimination of slavery, child labor and various forms of prejudice against women. During the past 15 years, we have attempted to meet the needs of the poor and underprivileged of our nation to such an extent as to claim from every healthy wage earner taxes for another one-third of a person. We have recently stood up and decried the nuclear arms race by the thousands. We are still far from a social incarnation of the reign of God, but we have made progress, and Christianity lies at the heart of many of the changes which have taken place.

A word here must be said about socialistic countries and their role in the building of the reign of God.

During the past century, socialism has spread throughout the world, manifesting a different look in various countries, to be sure. Socialists attempt to sketch on paper what a just society ought to look like, and then govern the peoples accordingly. Governments like those in the U.S.S.R. and China are so determined to make the social reality conform to the paper blueprints as to practice genocide and the worst forms of oppression. But the reign of God cannot be forced upon us; we must grow into it. It is tempting to see in socialism the best example of what the reign of God ought to look like, but history has demonstrated most unambiguously that socialism will not work in a spiritually bankrupt country. Socialism presupposes a level of altruism that only Christianity can make happen, but where such a Christian culture would exist, even laissez-faire capitalism would work well without oppressing the disadvantaged.

One of the important ways in which the reign of God becomes manifest in society is through the prophetic voice for human rights. At the cutting edge of the transformation of social conscience are the prophets of the reign of God—those men and women who put themselves on the line by standing up for what they believe to be true, just and charitable. The prophet is the one who makes others aware of opportunities to advance justice and peace, provoking a response from others. Because of prophets, the status quo is never allowed to ripen into a golden age of some sort. It is the mark of a healthy society that the voices of its prophets are allowed to be heard. Censoring, torturing and even killing the prophets of the kingdom only delays the fullness of its coming among us.

Even if one is not a Christian, the influence of

prophets will eventually touch the conscience. Leo Tolstoy wrote about a young man who professed to be an atheist, but who refused to submit to military conscription. He pointed out that the rationale employed by the young man—unwillingness to kill, love for the enemy and abhorrence of war—ultimately derived from Christianity. Many humanistic atheists might not agree with this interpretation, but there is little doubt that Christianity has colored the values of even the most strident atheists. The truths which humanists hold to be self-evident about human rights might never have achieved focus without Christianity.

The End Times

Since the Second World War, we have observed the emergence of a sense of global identity and consciousness—witness the United Nations and the proliferation of communications satellites. During this same period, the means to totally destroy our planet have been developed and multiplied and stored in nuclear weapons arsenals throughout the world. We have reached a critical stage in the history of planet earth; the future depends entirely on our ability to avoid war and to get along with one another. Glory and nothingness stare us in the face; there seems to be no middle ground.

Christianity believes that human society is moving toward the fulfillment of what has already begun in Christ: the elevation of human nature to a more intense involvement in the life of God. The Christian might not be able to outline the precise shape of the politics and economics of the ultimate, humanizing society, and he or she might not know how or when its emergence will be fully validated, but the Christian believes nonetheless that *Christ leads the way into the future and works with humanity as we grope to shape our world.* Marxists and secular humanists recognize no divine influence calling humanity toward any kind of fulfillment; to them, randomness and luck have characterized evolution all along the way, and it is entirely possible that the human venture will be shown up as an evolutionary dead end.

Christianity is not without its own intimations of doomsday, however. There are, among scripture scholars today, two very different viewpoints about how the reign of God will become established on earth. One viewpoint has it that God will have to intervene in a dramatic way, perhaps before we completely blow ourselves assunder. There will follow a judgment, whereafter the self-indulgent will be banished from the earth, allowing for the beginning of an age of unprecedented peace and prosperity. This perspective is most enthusiastically endorsed by various fundamentalist evangelicals, many of whom claim to know the precise pattern of events which will occur. The other viewpoint emphasizes a gradual transformation of societies, but not without catastrophes. Through wars and earthquakes and famines and plagues we shall persevere as Christ spins his web of love among us, finally establishing his spiritual headship among us through the quiet influence of loving people.

No matter what one believes about the end times, Christians are called to act here and now to make the reign of God a living reality. The future is God's, and we shall all die anyway. Better to work hard for the sake of love and let God worry about the Second Coming, if there is to be one during our lifetime.

Hope for the Future

The reign of God is furthered every time an individual reaches out in love and self-sacrifice to another; it advances at quantum leaps when genuine prophets speak out for justice and peace. But the threat of nuclear devastation casts a shadow over much of our work, reducing human efforts toward betterment to the level of total absurdity. Many today are losing heart because of the nuclear threat. Even Christians are finding that work in the present seems just a charade if there is no future into which we might hook our present hopes and dreams. Without a future, we are left only with the present moment, which we exploit fitfully for every smidgeon of pleasure we can extract from it. Never before in history have we so needed prophets of hope and lovers of humanity; never have voices of pessimism and selfishness been so loud.

Christianity alone, out of all the world's religions and systems of thought, is capable of sustaining hope in a nuclear age. Without this hope we shall lose heart completely. Hope is the substrate and progenitor of all creative human efforts; hope precedes faith, giving it direction and energy; charity cannot become enflamed without hope, suffocating in its absence. Although reasons to despair loom before us day and night, Christianity still affirms that the one who was crucified—who bore the brunt of human wickedness and the forces of evil—has already overcome the most insidious obstacles to human growth and social progress. Hope shall bear fruit.

"Jesus is risen," proclaims the church. If this is true, then he is the Lord of life and death. His will is sovereign, his power is certain, his ability to keep his promises is assured. History shall not result in a complete reversal of the process of humanization which has been proceeding for thousands of years. The creative Power behind evolution will prevail. Humankind has a future.

Perhaps it is here, concerning the issue of hope, that we can most appreciate the significance of the resurrection of Jesus. Perhaps the carpenter from Galilee is our only hope for survival, not to mention prosperity and peace. Perhaps . . . but how shall we know unless we take him at his word?

Appendix One
Questions for Reflection and Discussion

Chapter One: The Witness of the Church
1. Why did the apostles believe in the resurrection of Jesus?
2. How do you feel about the discrepancies among the resurrection narratives?
3. What kinds of qualities in people help you to trust in their words?
4. Why are some people so threatened by the advances of science?
5. Do you believe Jesus rose from the dead? Explain.

Chapter Two: Incarnation
1. Why are there so many different notions about what God is like?
2. Do you believe people can know anything about God?
3. What are some of the most surprising qualities of God revealed by Jesus?
4. What are some of the pitfalls to growth that come with riches and health?
5. What does the incarnation mean to you?

Chapter Three: New Life
1. Why did the apostles emphasize the resurrection as the core of the gospel?

2. Why do some people choose not to believe in the resurrection?
3. What is the relationship between the resurrection and pentecost?
4. Do you believe you have met the risen Christ in your life? Explain.

Chapter Four: The Mystical Body

1. How did Paul's conversion experience influence his theology of church?
2. How do you feel about organized religion? About authority in the church?
3. Why is it important for a Christian to be part of a church?
4. What are some of the ways in which you benefit from community involvement?

Chapter Five: When Good Things Happen to Bad People

1. How do you feel about the prosperity of wicked people?
2. In what ways does the Christian doctrine of judgment contribute to peace?
3. How do you feel about the prospect of giving God an accounting of your life?
4. Do you believe some people will really go to hell? Explain.
5. Why are the decisions we make each day so important?

Chapter Six: Courage to Live

1. How do you feel about the prospect of your own death?
2. How does belief in the resurrection help to cope with the fear of death?

3. Do you believe non-Christians suffer more from their fear of death?

4. Do you believe your dead loved ones still live in the presence of God?

Chapter Seven: The Meaning of Suffering

1. From what kinds of pains do you suffer most?

2. Do you believe God is responsible for human suffering? Explain.

3. How does Christianity help people to find meaning in suffering?

4. In what ways do certain platitudes contribute to unredemptive suffering?

Chapter Eight: Meaning in Life

1. Why are universal principles such powerful motivators?

2. How does Christian growth differ from the Buddhist approach?

3. How does Christian growth differ from secular humanism's challenges?

4. In what ways does Jesus clarify the meaning of truth, love and justice?

5. What, to you, is the most important thing in the world?

Chapter Nine: The Reign of God

1. Do you believe God would allow humanity to suffer nuclear holocaust?

2. Why are Christian prophets so unpopular?

3. What are some of the signs of the emergence of God's reign?

4. What does the Second Coming of Christ mean to you?

5. Why is it inappropriate for a Christian to ever despair of life?

Appendix Two
Suggested Reading

A New Catechism: Catholic Faith for Adults (New York, NY: Crossroad, 1977). See sections concerning the resurrection.

Brown, Raymond: *The Virginal Conception and Bodily Resurrection of Jesus* (Mahwah, NJ: Paulist Press, 1973).

Brown, Raymond, Joseph A. Fitzmeyer and Roland E. Murphy, Editors: *The Jerome Biblical Commentary* (Englewood Cliffs, NJ: Prentice-Hall, 1968). See commentaries on resurrection narratives.

Dulles, Avery: *Apologetics and the Biblical Christ* (Westminster, MD: Newman Press, 1967).

Jones, Alexander, Editor: *The Jerusalem Bible* (New York, NY: Doubleday, 1966). The introductions to the New Testament books and the footnotes in the text are very helpful.

Kung, Hans: *On Being a Christian* (New York, NY: Doubleday, 1976). This discussion of the resurrection narratives is rich in its scripture scholarship.

Lohfink, Gerhard: *The Last Day of Jesus* (Notre Dame, IN: Ave Maria Press, 1984).

McKenzie, John L.: *The Power and the Glory* (Milwaukee, WI: Bruce, 1965).
Dictionary of the Bible (New York, NY: Macmillan, 1965). See especially the entries concerning Jesus, resurrection, body, soul and spirit.

Merton, Thomas: *He Is Risen* (Niles, IL: Argus Communications, 1975).

Purcell, William: *The Resurrection* (Philadelphia, PA: Westminster Press, 1966). A dialogue between two prominent Protestant theologians.

Rahner, Carl, S.J., and Herbert Vorgrimler: *Dictionary of Theology* (New York, NY: Crossroad, 1981).

U.S. Catholic Conference: *The Kung Dialogue* (Washington, D.C., 1980). Includes several penetrating exchanges between Professor Kung and the Catholic Magisterium concerning the nature of the resurrection.